D0583594

The Alamo
Symbol of Freedom

Patriotic Symbols of America

The Alamo
Symbol of Freedom

Hal Marcovitz

Mason Crest
Philadelphia

Mason Crest
450 Parkway Drive, Suite D
Broomall, PA 19008
www.masoncrest.com

© 2015 by Mason Crest, an imprint of National Highlights, Inc.

Printed and bound in the United States of America.

CPSIA Compliance Information: Batch #PSA2014. For further information, contact Mason Crest at 1-866-MCP-Book.

Publisher's note: all quotations in this book come from original sources, and contain the spelling and grammatical inconsistencies of the original text.

First printing
1 3 5 7 9 8 6 4 2

Library of Congress Cataloging-in-Publication Data

on file at the Library of Congress

ISBN: 978-1-4222-3118-0 (hc)
ISBN: 978-1-4222-8741-5 (ebook)

Patriotic Symbols of America series ISBN: 978-1-4222-3117-3

Contents

KEY ICONS TO LOOK FOR:

Text-dependent questions: These questions send the reader back to the text for more careful attention to the evidence presented there.

Words to understand: These words with their easy-to-understand definitions will increase the reader's understanding of the text, while building vocabulary skills.

Series glossary of key terms: This back-of-the book glossary contains terminology used throughout this series. Words found here increase the reader's ability to read and comprehend higher-level books and articles in this field.

Research projects: Readers are pointed toward areas of further inquiry connected to each chapter. Suggestions are provided for projects that encourage deeper research and analysis.

Sidebars: This boxed material within the main text allows readers to build knowledge, gain insights, explore possibilities, and broaden their perspectives by weaving together additional information to provide realistic and holistic perspectives.

Patriotic Symbols and American History

Symbols are not merely ornaments to admire—they also tell us stories. If you look at one of them closely, you may want to find out why it was made and what it truly means. If you ask people who live in the society in which the symbol exists, you will learn some things. But by studying the people who created that symbol and the reasons why they made it, you will understand the deepest meanings of that symbol.

The United States owes its identity to great events in history, and the most remarkable of our patriotic symbols are rooted in these events. The struggle for independence from Great Britain gave America the Declaration of Independence, the Liberty Bell, the American flag, and other images of freedom. The War of 1812 gave the young country a song dedicated to the flag, "The Star-Spangled Banner," which became our national anthem. Nature gave the country its national animal, the bald eagle. These symbols established the identity of the new nation, and set it apart from the nations of the Old World.

To be emotionally moving, a symbol must strike people with a sense of power and unity. But it often takes a long time for a new symbol to be accepted by all the people, especially if there are older symbols that have gradually lost popularity. For example, the image of Uncle Sam has replaced Brother Jonathan, an earlier representation of the national will, while the Statue of Liberty has replaced Columbia, a woman who represented liberty to Americans in the early 19th century. Since then, Uncle Sam and the Statue of Liberty have endured and have become cherished icons of America.

Of all the symbols, the Statue of Liberty has perhaps the most curious story, for unlike other symbols, Americans did not create her. She was created by the French, who then gave her to America. Hence, she represented not what Americans thought of their country but rather what the French thought of America. It was many years before Americans decided to accept this French goddess of Liberty as a symbol for the United States and its special role among the nations: to spread freedom and enlighten the world.

This series of books is valuable because it presents the story of each of America's great symbols in a freshly written way and will contribute to the students' knowledge and awareness of them. It it to be hoped that this information will awaken an abiding interest in American history, as well as in the meanings of American symbols.

— Barry Moreno,
librarian and historian
Ellis Island/Statue of Liberty National Monument

 Words to Understand

Congress—the lawmaking branch of the United States government.

homestead—the home and adjoining land owned and occupied by a family.

pelt—animal hide.

president—leader of a government selected by popular vote.

The frontiersman Davy Crockett remains a popular and mythic figures of American history. Crockett was famed as an outdoorsman because of his crack shooting. He named his long rifle "Old Betsy." The rifle was presented to him as a gift, and the inscription on the barrel reads: "Go Ahead."

Davy Crockett

By 1835, Davy Crockett was a living American folk hero. As an Indian fighter, Crockett served under General Andrew Jackson and helped defeat the Creek Indians in Alabama and Florida. His exploits as a pioneer were also well known to the thousands of readers of the "Crockett Almanacs"—short, easy-to-read books that told about Davy's adventures exploring the mountains of his native Tennessee. It did not seem to matter to his devoted fans that Crockett and his ghost writers made up most of the stories contained in the almanacs. His readers hungered for the tall tales and backwoods humor of the man who dressed in buckskins, carried a rifle he called "Old Betsy," and wore a hat fashioned from a raccoon *pelt*.

As for Crockett, he used his fame as a frontiersman to help boost his political career. In 1821, he was elected to the state legislature in Tennessee. Six years later he won election to the United States House of Representatives. There was no question that Crockett was a rising star in *Congress*. Many political insiders in Washington expected Crockett to make a bid for the presidency.

Crockett encouraged such talk. In 1834, he made secret plans to begin campaigning for the Whig Party nomination for the 1836 presidential election. One man who suspected Crockett's plans was his old military commander, Andrew Jackson, now the *president*. A Democrat, Jackson won his first term in 1828 and had been reelected in 1832. Now, Jackson wanted his vice president, Martin Van Buren, to win the election of 1836 and take office as president. Van Buren would continue Jackson's policies.

Make Connections

Davy Crockett once served under General Andrew Jackson, but by the time Crockett was in Congress and Jackson was president, Crockett disliked his old commander so much that he would boast to other lawmakers: "Look at my neck and you will not find any collar with a label, 'My Dog, Andrew Jackson.'"

Crockett had split with his old commander on many issues, including the Indian Removal Bill—a law that enabled the U.S. Army to push thousands of Indians off their lands so that those lands could be settled by white pioneers. Crockett had befriended many Indians during his days as a frontiersman and claimed to owe his life to Indians who saved him from starvation on the trail.

Crockett was in the minority, however. Most Americans supported the Indian Removal Bill. Whenever Crockett spoke against the bill, he angered not only Andrew Jackson but also the voters back home in Tennessee, many of whom had lost friends and relatives to Indian attacks while trying to establish their *homesteads* in the early years of the 19th century.

As the congressional elections of 1835 approached, Jackson and the Democrats aimed to rid themselves of Davy Crockett. For Crockett's seat in Congress, they supported a Tennessee lawyer named Adam Huntsman.

The two men crisscrossed Tennessee, campaigning hard for votes. Crockett ultimately lost in a close vote—he received 4,400 votes, 250 less than Huntsman. Now out of Congress, Davy Crockett was no longer a threat to run against Van Buren in the presidential election.

Crockett felt bitter about losing the election. He found it hard to believe the rural folks in Tennessee had turned him out of office. He declared that he planned to go back to the frontier life.

He headed for Texas.

Text-Dependent Question
Why were many Americans familiar with Davy Crockett in the 1830s?

Research Project
Write a report describing the impact of the Indian Removal Bill on Native Americans, and explain how this law contributed to U.S. expansion during the 19th century.

Words to Understand

agitator—a person who stirs up public feeling on controversial issues.

constitution—the laws of a nation, usually presented in written form and adopted by a nation's government.

dictator—a leader of a government who exerts absolute control, usually without consent of the people.

garrison—a body of troops, usually assigned to hold a fort.

immigrant—a person that comes to a different country to take up permanent residence.

mission—a settlement established by Spanish priests in the American southwest, from which they could carry out their work of converting the Native Americans to Christianity.

siege—a military blockade of a city or fort, in order to force it to surrender.

Stephen F. Austin created this map of the province of Texas in 1822. In 1821 Austin and his father, Moses, led a group of Americans to Texas and received permission from the Mexican government to settle there. The map, drawn on cloth and labeled in Spanish, shows where the Americans settled in the eastern part of Texas, along the Gulf of Mexico.

"Come and Take It"

In the 1600s and 1700s, the Spaniards established *missions* across the Southwest. They were small, walled villages composed of churches, trading posts, and hospitals. One of the missions was erected in 1723 just outside the Texas farming town of San Antonio.

By the early 1800s, the mission at San Antonio was no longer serving as a church. Instead, the Spanish army used it as a fort. The soldiers called it the Alamo in honor of their hometown in Mexico, Alamo de Parras. In Spanish, the word *alamo* means "cottonwood," which is a type of tree common to the region.

Although Spain controlled large amounts of land— they claimed territory as far west as the Pacific coast of

Make Connections

The name Texas comes from the Caddo Indian word *tejas*, which means "friends."

California—the government of Spain did not care very much about its possessions north of the Rio Grande River. This is a long waterway that today separates modern Mexico from the United States. Few Spaniards wanted to live in this area.

Eventually, American settlers in search of cheap land found their way west and established homesteads in Texas. Moses Austin and his son, Stephen F. Austin, arrived in Texas in 1821, establishing a homestead between the Brazos and Colorado Rivers. Moses Austin approached the Spanish government for permission to stake out an American colony in the rough Texas landscape, but died before receiving approval. His son continued his efforts, but before he received permission for the new colony he learned that the Spaniards would no longer be making decisions for Mexico. In 1821, Mexico won its independence from Spain.

Austin soon found himself dealing with a number of government representatives. None of them remained in power long enough to give Austin permission to establish an American colony.

Finally, in 1824, Austin received permission for 300 American families to stake

Make Connections

Mission San Antonio de Valero is the actual name of the Spanish mission that came to be known as the Alamo

out a colony along the Colorado and Brazos Rivers in the southeastern portion of Texas. The Texans settled down to their new lives as farmers.

Over the next few years, 8,000 pioneers willing to leave America and become Mexican citizens followed "The Old Three Hundred" to Texas, lured by the promise of cheap land. By 1830 some 75 percent of the population of Texas was composed of *immigrants* from America.

Early in 1831, William Barret Travis arrived in Texas and started a law practice in Anáhuac, a port town on Galveston Bay. He obtained a land grant from Austin. Travis soon became involved with a group of *agitators* known as the "War Party." Travis and the others wanted to be free of Mexico's rule. They were willing to fight

VITAL FIGURE: Stephen F. Austin

Stephen Fuller Austin was born in Virginia and educated at schools in Connecticut and Kentucky. In 1821 he followed his father Moses to Texas to help establish an American colony. When Moses Austin died, Stephen led 300 families—known as "The Old Three Hundred"—to settle on the banks of the Colorado and Brazos Rivers.

When Mexico won its independence, Austin became the chief diplomat for the Texans, attempting to negotiate resolutions to their grievances with the Mexicans. For his efforts, though, Santa Anna had him thrown in jail.

Following the Texas War for Independence, Austin became the Texas Republic's first secretary of state, but died shortly after assuming office in 1836. Nevertheless, his efforts to win independence for Texas earned him his place in history as the "Father of Texas." The state's capital city, Austin, is named for him.

against the Mexican government to win their freedom.

Tensions between the Texans and the Mexicans were increasing. During a trip to Mexico City in January 1833, Stephen F. Austin found the new Mexican leader, Antonio López de Santa Anna, concerned more about the internal problems of his government than negotiating with the Texans over their grievances.

Make Connections

The first hospital in Texas was established inside the walls of the Alamo in the early 1800s by Spanish military doctors.

As a compromise, Austin proposed to Mexican Vice President Valentine Gomez Farias that Texas become a Mexican state. Farias dismissed Austin's suggestion, taking it more as a threat than a compromise. When Austin urged settlers in San Antonio to form their own government, Santa Anna had him arrested. He remained in a Mexican jail for 18 months.

With Austin in prison, agitators in Texas remained quiet, fearing that if they caused trouble Santa Anna would have Austin executed. Meanwhile, in Mexico City, Santa Anna—who had come to power in a democratic election—abolished the country's *constitution* and declared himself *dictator* of Mexico.

Austin was released from jail in late 1835. In the meantime, Texans had formed the rowdy, ragtag "Volunteer Army of Texas" under General Sam Houston. Travis was given the rank of colonel and appointed to head a *garrison*.

The first shots in the Texas War for Independence were fired on October 1, 1835. Mexican troops under the command of General Martín Perfecto de Cós arrived in the town of Gonzales and ordered the settlers to turn over their cannon. The settlers responded by hoisting a flag over the cannon bearing the words: "Come and Take It."

VITAL FIGURE: Mexican ruler Santa Anna

Antonio López de Santa Anna, who considered himself the "Napoleon of the West," was born in Xalapa in the Mexican state of Veracruz in 1794. He chose the military as a career, becoming an infantry cadet at the age of 16. As a young soldier, he often displayed valor on the battlefield and quickly moved up in rank. By the age of 22, he had achieved the rank of captain.

In 1821, as Mexicans were fighting for their independence, Santa Anna was in charge of government forces defending the city of Orizaba. During an attack by the Mexican rebels, he switched sides and helped the rebels defeat forces loyal to Spain. When Spain gave Mexico its freedom, Santa Anna became a powerful military leader. He used the army to overthrow Agustin de Iturbide, who had declared himself emperor of Mexico. The country returned to a democracy. Now a popular leader, Santa Anna was elected president in 1831.

Democracy wouldn't last long. Santa Anna declared himself dictator and ruled Mexico with an iron will until 1836, when he was captured by Sam Houston at the Battle of San Jacinto. Following his return to Mexico, he remained in office, even after losing the Mexican War and along with it vast amounts of territory to the United States. He was finally driven from office in 1854 by reformer Benito Juárez.

Santa Anna died quietly in bed in 1876 at age 82.

Make Connections

A "maverick" is someone who is independent mind-ed, and often stands against authority; the word owes its inclusion in the English language to Sam Maverick, an Alamo defender. Maverick did not die at the Alamo; he left the mission in early March of 1836 to represent the defenders at the Texas con-stitutional convention.

Cós and his men moved against the settlers. The Texans shot back, easily dri-ving off Cós and his troops. The Mexicans were forced to flee to San Antonio, where they were pursued by Texas troops under the command of Colonel Benjamin Milam. Cós and his men took refuge in the Alamo. After a five-day *siege*, General Cós surrendered. Humiliated, the Mexicans marched out of Texas.

The Texans were now in control of the old Spanish mission.

Santa Anna erupted in anger and personally led an army of 5,500 soldiers north toward San Antonio.

Meanwhile, Travis arrived in San Antonio and took command of the troops that had driven off Cós. Also arriving in San Antonio was Colonel Jim Bowie, who had been sent by Sam Houston. Finally, on February 8, 1836, Davy Crockett and a dozen fron-tiersmen from Tennessee rode into San Antonio. There were now roughly

Make Connections

Mexican soldiers wore hats known as "shakos"—caps shaped like cylinders with tiny front bills. During the chaos of battle, Santa Anna insisted that "all shako chin-straps will be correctly worn—these the com-manders will watch closely."

150 men occupying the Alamo, awaiting Santa Anna's army of 5,500 soldiers.

In a few short days, William Travis, Jim Bowie and Davy Crockett would lead one of history's most heroic stands against overwhelming odds.

 Text-Dependent Question
Who were the "Old Three Hundred"?

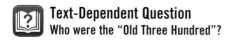 **Research Project**
Do some research in the library, and list the causes of the Mexican War for Independence (1810-1821). Explain how gaining independence made Mexico an appealing destination for immigrant settlers like Moses and Stephen Austin.

 # Words to Understand

artillery—large guns, such as cannons, used by a military force.

bayonets—long knives mounted on the ends of rifle barrels.

bombardment—a vigorous artillery attack.

casualties—a soldier lost to his unit because he has been killed, wounded, or captured.

emissaries—representatives of a nation dispatched to talk to another nation's representatives.

morale—the level of enthusiasm or loyalty of a group with regard to a task at hand.

mutiny—the desire of troops to overthrow their leader.

viva—in Spanish, an exclamation translated to "Long live." It is used to express good will or approval.

Davy Crockett, out of ammunition, swings his rifle at attacking Mexican soldiers in this painting of the Alamo defenders. Santa Anna attacked the fort with thousands of Mexican soldiers; the defenders numbered just 183 men.

"Victory or Death"

Jim Bowie was a stocky, mean-tempered, and sandy-haired man. He was known to be as quick with his fists as he was with the large, double-edged knife strapped to his hip. Now, Bowie found himself soldiering under the command of Sam Houston, who sent him to San Antonio to burn down the Alamo.

Houston feared the mission could fall back into Mexican hands. After spending a few days at the Alamo, Bowie found himself impressed with the defenders—he concluded they were brave, headstrong men willing to place their lives on the line for Texas independence. And he was also convinced the old mission was the key to the defense of Texas. He sent word back to Houston that if

VITAL FIGURE: William Travis

William Barret Travis was just 26 years old when he took command of the 183 men who defended the Alamo. Born in South Carolina in 1809, the eldest of 11 children, Travis settled in Alabama and opened a practice as a lawyer, but left quickly for Texas in 1831. It is believed he fled Alabama after killing a man.

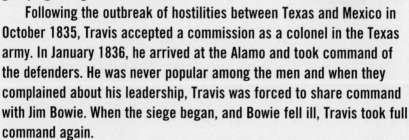

After arriving in Texas he found himself caught up in the movement for independence and became a leader of the "War Party," the group agitating for armed revolt.

Following the outbreak of hostilities between Texas and Mexico in October 1835, Travis accepted a commission as a colonel in the Texas army. In January 1836, he arrived at the Alamo and took command of the defenders. He was never popular among the men and when they complained about his leadership, Travis was forced to share command with Jim Bowie. When the siege began, and Bowie fell ill, Travis took full command again.

Santa Anna could be turned back at the Alamo, victory would be theirs. "We will rather die in these ditches than give it up to the enemy," Bowie wrote.

By February 10, Santa Anna's army had reached the Rio Grande, just 150 miles southwest of the Alamo. Meanwhile, squabbling broke out among the defenders at the Alamo. Travis had never been popular among the men. Sensing he could have a *mutiny* on his hands, Travis reluctantly agreed to an election to name a commander. Bowie won the vote and, wishing to avoid trouble, offered to share command with Travis.

By February 23, Santa Anna's men had advanced to within a few miles of San Antonio. That night, the first of Santa Anna's troops arrived in San Antonio. They raised the Mexican flag over San Fernando Church. Bowie sent two *emissaries* out to meet the Mexicans. They returned a short time later with Santa Anna's terms: The Texans were expected to make a complete and unconditional surrender. Travis answered that message with a message

VITAL FIGURE: Jim Bowie

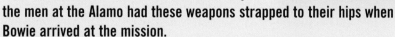

James Bowie was born in Kentucky in 1796. He led a colorful life as a smuggler, slave trader, mustang roper, bear hunter, alligator wrestler and soldier.

In 1826, Bowie started carrying a large, doubled-edged butcher knife strapped to his hip. On September 19, 1827, Bowie was involved in a duel near Natchez, Mississippi. During the fight, Norris Wright, the local sheriff, shot Bowie in the chest; when Wright advanced on Bowie to finish him off, Bowie drew his long knife and plunged it into Wright's chest. The knife Bowie used to kill Wright earned the name "Bowie knife." From that day forward, fighting men across the country armed themselves with Bowie knives. Many of the men at the Alamo had these weapons strapped to their hips when Bowie arrived at the mission.

Sam Houston sent Bowie to the Alamo to burn it down, but Bowie believed that if the Texans could stop the Mexicans in San Antonio, victory would be theirs. However, Bowie fell ill at the start of the siege and had little to do with repelling the Mexican attacks; he died in bed from a bayonet attack when Mexican soldiers stormed into the Alamo.

of his own—a blast from an Alamo cannon.

The Mexican siege began at dawn the next morning. Some 400 yards from the Alamo, down by the banks of the San Antonio River, the Mexicans rolled out three cannons and commenced a steady *artillery bombardment* on the mission. The shells caused little damage.

However, the defenders were without their commander. For weeks, Bowie had been growing ill. On February 24, he was so sick with fever that he could not stand. He was carried to his bunk and Travis assumed complete command of the garrison. That night, Travis composed a message to the people of Texas. It read:

> Fellow citizens and compatriots, I am besieged by a thousand or more of the Mexicans under Santa Anna. I have sustained a continual bombardment and cannonade for 24 hours and have not lost a man. The enemy has demanded a surrender at discretion, otherwise, the garrison are to be put to the sword, if the fort is taken. I have answered the demand with a cannon shot, and our flag still waves proudly from the walls. I shall never surrender or retreat. Then, I call on you in the name of liberty, of patriotism and everything dear to the American character, to come to our aid, with all dispatch. The enemy is receiving reinforcements daily and will no doubt increase to three or four thousand in four or five days. If this call is neglected, I am determined to sustain myself as long as possible and die like a soldier who never forgets what is due to his honor and that of his country—Victory or Death.

The message was given to a rider, who was sent to the town of Gonzales, 65 miles east of San Antonio. Travis and the Alamo defenders hoped reinforcements were waiting there.

The Mexicans continued the siege on February 25. This time, they tried to storm the walls of the mission, but were easily driven back. The defenders killed several Mexican soldiers, but had not yet suffered *casualties* themselves. Davy Crockett led the defense of the mission during the attack.

Meanwhile, reinforcements headed toward San Antonio. One garrison of 300 Texans led by Colonel

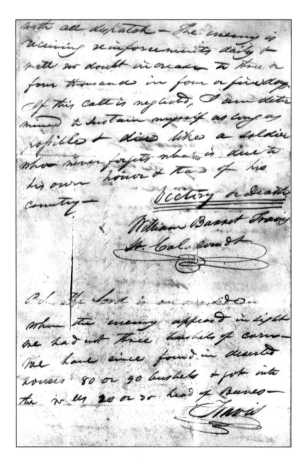

The final page of William Travis's February 24 letter from the Alamo is signed "Victory or Death." The outnumbered Alamo defenders hoped that Texan reinforcements would arrive in time to end the siege by Santa Anna's Mexican troops.

James Fannin got within 90 miles of the mission, but stalled when wagons broke down and oxen wandered away. Fannin decided to turn back and return to his fort at Goliad. A smaller group based in Gonzales made it to the Alamo; they sneaked through Mexican lines and entered the fort in the early morning hours of March 1. They were welcomed, to be sure, but the troops from Gonzales merely added 25 soldiers to the ranks of the defenders.

By now, Santa Anna had moved his cannons within 250 yards of the mission walls. He kept up a constant bombardment. The bursts of shells against the old mission were damaging the Alamo walls as well as the *morale* of the defenders. To many of the Texans inside the Alamo, it appeared the end was near.

On the afternoon of March 5, Travis called the defenders into the plaza of the Alamo and told them reinforcements would not be coming. Travis said that he intended to stay in the mission and defend it to the death. The colonel told the men they had his permission to leave. All but one man chose to stay. That night, a Frenchman, Louis Rose, climbed over the wall. He was never seen again.

Unknown to the Texans, Santa Anna was organizing the final assault on the fort. He planned to send 1,100 men against four walls of the fort in a raid staged early the next morning. Just before dawn, the Texans heard the cry: *"Viva* Santa Anna!"

The chaos inside the Alamo walls can be seen in this painting, titled "Dawn at the Alamo." On the north wall (at right), fort commander William Travis fires his pistol at an attacker. Travis was killed defending the wall.

A bugle sounded the call to attack.

Hundreds of Mexicans suddenly rose up out of the darkness and stormed the Alamo, throwing makeshift ladders against the mission's stone walls. Travis had been asleep in his quarters. He awoke, grabbed his sword and commanded the Texans to repel the attack. "The Mexicans are upon us and we'll give them hell!" he shouted.

Travis died minutes later. He had rushed to the defense of the north wall, where he was killed by a single bullet.

Make Connections

Some 650 Mexicans were killed in the Battle of the Alamo, but not all of them were killed by the defenders. It is believed many Mexicans were killed by "friendly fire," meaning they were shot by errant blasts from their own lines.

Weak with fever, Jim Bowie lay in bed, gripping pistols in his weak hands. Suddenly, the door of his room crashed open and Mexican soldiers flooded in. Bowie fired into the crowd of soldiers. He stopped a few of them, but others made it to his bedside and fell on him with their *bayonets*.

Davy Crockett commanded about 100 troops stationed along the southern wall. Hundreds of Mexican soldiers suddenly appeared at the base of the wall; within seconds, Crockett's men were overwhelmed by the advance of the Mexicans. The defenders were forced to fight in hand-to-hand combat against the Mexicans.

There is controversy about how Davy Crockett died. Susannah Dickinson, the wife of one of the Alamo defenders, later said that she saw "Colonel Crockett lying dead and mutilated between the church and the two-story barracks." Other sources say Crockett and six of his men knew the fight was hopeless, and they surrendered to a Mexican officer named

Make Connections

Alamo defender Brigido Guerrero was the only man who escaped with his life from the mission. He convinced Santa Anna's troops that he was a Mexican who had been held prisoner by the Texans. He was released unharmed.

Manuel Castrillón, who promised to spare their lives.

By then, Santa Anna had arrived at the Alamo. He was angry that it had cost the lives of more than 600 Mexican soldiers to defeat 183 defenders in the mission.

> ### Make Connections
>
> Davy Crockett probably wore his coonskin cap during the final battle; Susannah Dickinson reported later that she saw Crockett's "peculiar cap" lying next to his dead body.

Castrillón marched his prisoners to Santa Anna and informed the dictator that he captured the "naturalist Davy Crockett, well-known in North America for his unusual adventures." He asked Santa Anna to spare the prisoners, but the dictator would show no mercy. He ordered the immediate executions of the survivors. Several Mexican officers drew their swords and cut the men down.

The bodies of the slain defenders were burned in the Alamo plaza.

Susannah Dickinson was among 10 women and children found hiding in the Alamo church. They were all released by Santa Anna, who told her to tell the people of Texas all she had seen that day.

Text-Dependent Questions
How many Texans defended the Alamo? How many survived the battle?

Research Project
Read the diary of José Enrique de la Peña, a Mexican officer who was present at the Alamo. Then do some research into the diary's origins to find out more about the controversy over how Davy Crockett died. Explain what you believe to be the true story, using evidence to support your conclusion.

Words to Understand

adobe—sun-dried mud used to make bricks.

artifacts—man-made objects, usually serving as reminders of an important event or place.

centennial—the 100th anniversary of an event.

facade—the decorative front of a building.

hallowed—holy, consecrated, sacred, or revered.

porcelain—baked clay used to make plates and other dinnerware.

Night falls over San Antonio and the Alamo. Today the Alamo is one of the most popular tourist attractions in Texas. The city of San Antonio has grown up around the old Spanish mission, which remains a symbol of Texas independence.

The Shrine of Texas Liberty

The Alamo was composed of a large rectangular plaza of about three acres. The stone walls were from nine to 12 feet high and three feet thick. The gates could be found in the south wall. The barracks were located along the east and west walls and fashioned from *adobe*. Along the east wall, the men lived in a large two-story structure known as the Long Barracks.

At one time, the Alamo contained a church, because the mission's original function was as a place of worship. But the roof of the church collapsed in the 1760s. When Bowie took command of the garrison, he ordered the roof repaired.

It is the arched entrance to the church, featuring four

decorative stone columns, that most people recognize as the familiar symbol of the Alamo.

Military historians have looked back on the Battle of the Alamo and concluded that the Texans would have had a better chance of survival had the Alamo been smaller. The sprawling compound of buildings with walls as long as football fields was too large for a force of 183 men to defend. Travis had just 20 cannons to defend the walls; he was forced to spread out his big guns and was unable to use them effectively to repel the Mexican assaults.

Following the admission of Texas as a state in 1845, the U.S. Army took over the Alamo and used it as a fort until the Civil War. Texas entered the Union as a slave state and joined the Confederacy in 1861. The army returned briefly following the Civil War, but in 1876 the soldiers left for good when the army opened Fort Sam Houston in San Antonio. The *San Antonio Daily Express* suggested then that the state of Texas should assume ownership of the Alamo, but the idea failed to attract much interest among state officials.

In 1877, Honore Grenet, a French-born San Antonio merchant, purchased the Long Barracks and took a lease out on the chapel, opening his general store in the quarters that once housed the Alamo's brave defenders. He ran advertisements in local newspapers urging his patrons to "Remember the Alamo—Shop at Grenet's."

Grenet died in 1881. His heirs sold the business to

In the years after the battle, the Alamo buildings served many purposes. The old fort was occupied during the Civil War, then it was used as a store, and later as a warehouse. During the 1880s a museum was established in the Alamo's chapel; the entire property was purchased in 1905, so that it could be used as a museum. Here, visitors walk outside the entrance to the mission's church

Hugo & Schmeltzer, a warehouse company. The chapel was destined to serve as a warehouse until the city government of San Antonio stepped in and purchased it. The city ran the chapel as a museum for several years.

Finally, in 1905, the Texas Legislature set aside funds to buy the entire Alamo property and preserve it as a museum. The legislators entrusted the property to the Daughters of the Republic of Texas, a historical society. The Daughters have maintained the property since then, at no cost to the taxpayers, mostly by selling souvenirs to the 2.5 million tourists who visit the Alamo each year.

Souvenirs from the Alamo have always been popular; in fact, tourists started helping themselves to *artifacts* from the mission long before the property became a museum. Shortly after the battle, Texans wishing to hold on to mementos from the historic siege made off with cannonballs, discarded weapons and even chips from the stone walls.

By the late 1890s, *porcelain* plates and silver spoons bearing images of the Alamo were on sale in the museum's gift shop, and seemed to satisfy the desires of people in search of mementos from the mission. Some of the souvenirs were manufactured in Europe and Asia, others were fashioned at a factory right in San Antonio—the Alamo Iron Works.

By 1936—the *centennial* anniversary of Texas independence—the front *facade* of the Alamo church had become the most recognizable image in the state.

Once located outside the town limits, the Alamo can

The state flag of Texas, shown here, includes a single star. The Lone Star flag is a reminder of Texas's short history as an independent republic.

now be found in downtown San Antonio. Over the years, the city of San Antonio grew and eventually engulfed the battlefield where Santa Anna's army staged its attacks on the mission. In the time of Travis, Crockett, and Bowie, San Antonio was a sleepy farming town. Today, it is a busy metropolis with more than a million residents.

Nevertheless, the mission remains *hallowed* ground to the people of Texas, who regard the Alamo as the "Shrine of Texas Liberty."

Text-Dependent Question
What is the name of the organization that maintains the Alamo today?

Research Project
Using the photos in this book, supplemented with images from the Internet, create a model of the Alamo. A shoebox will make a good base for the chapel; cut off the lid and use it to create the building's facade. Use cardboard to make the walls. Cover the model with clay or construction paper, and paint to look like stonework. Flesh out your diorama with fake grass and toy soldiers to show how the building looked when it was being defended.

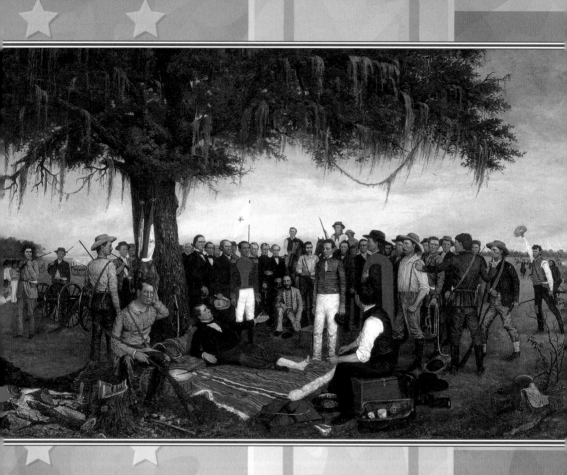

 Words to Understand

diplomacy—activity by officials of two or more nations who try to resolve their problems by talking and negotiating.

pyre—fuel used to burn in a funeral fire.

siesta—an afternoon nap.

The Texans would follow up the Alamo defeat with a smashing victory over Santa Anna's army just six weeks later at the Battle of San Jacinto. This 1886 painting by William Huddle depicts the surrender of Santa Anna. It pictures many of the leaders in the revolt for Texas independence, including Sam Houston (reclining under the tree). Santa Anna is near the center of the photo, wearing a green jacket and white pants.

"Remember the Alamo!"

Following the massacre at the mission, Santa Anna aimed to put down the Texas rebellion. He attacked Colonel James Fannin's troops at Goliad on March 27, slaughtering more than 300 Texans. But then, Santa Anna made a tactical error. He divided his army, and sent most of his men north in pursuit of other Texas rebels.

Sam Houston caught up with the Mexican dictator about six weeks after the battle of the Alamo. Near the plain of San Jacinto, Santa Anna found himself facing a force of 800 Texans under Sam Houston. Santa Anna's army included about 1,250 Mexican soldiers.

Late in the afternoon of April 21, Houston surprised the Mexicans with a sudden attack as they dozed during their afternoon *siestas*. "Remember the Alamo!" the Texans shouted as they advanced across the battlefield.

The Mexicans had little fight in them. They were exhausted from their long marches and frightened by the charge of the Texans. Nearly every Mexican soldier was killed or captured. One of the casualties in the battle was General Castrillón, who had pleaded for Crockett's life. Santa Anna managed to escape, but he was captured the next day.

The dictator was brought before Houston, who had been wounded in the leg during the fighting the day before. Santa Anna asked Houston to be "generous to the vanquished."

"You should have remembered that at the Alamo," Houston snapped back.

Santa Anna was held prisoner until November. While in Houston's custody, he was forced to order Mexico's troops to leave Texas and grant Texas its independence. The war was over. The Texans had won.

Houston was elected the first president of the Texas Republic. He asked President Andrew Jackson to admit Texas as a state in the Union. However, U.S. leaders were slow to respond. In the 1830s, slavery was emerging as an issue that divided the country. Texas wanted to enter the Union as a slave state. It would not be admitted to the Union until December 29, 1845.

In the meantime, America's relations with Mexico were strained. In Washington, lawmakers wanted America to expand, adding the Mexican-held territories of New Mexico and California to the United States. Texas also had an ongoing squabble with Mexico. Santa Anna, who had returned to power following his release, never recognized the Rio Grande River as the border between Mexico and Texas. Instead, Santa Anna insisted the bor-

VITAL FIGURE: Sam Houston

Sam Houston achieved success in public life long before he became a leader in the Texas War for Independence. Born in 1793 in Tennessee and educated as a lawyer, Houston served with valor during the War of 1812. He won a seat in Congress in 1823 and four years later won election as his state's governor.

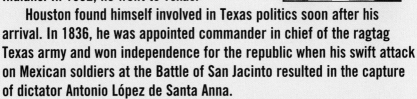

But Houston suffered from a troubled personal life. After his marriage broke up, he resigned as governor and went to live in the Tennessee mountains with the Cherokee Indians. In 1832, he went to Texas.

Houston found himself involved in Texas politics soon after his arrival. In 1836, he was appointed commander in chief of the ragtag Texas army and won independence for the republic when his swift attack on Mexican soldiers at the Battle of San Jacinto resulted in the capture of dictator Antonio López de Santa Anna.

He twice served as president of the Republic of Texas and supported statehood. After Texas' admission to the Union, Houston served as a U.S. senator and governor. In 1861, he was forced out of office as governor because he opposed his state's secession from the Union during the Civil War. He died at his home in Huntsville, Texas, in 1863.

Houston, Texas' largest city, is named after him.

American troops rout a Mexican army during the 1846 Mexican-American War. Although Texas had already won its freedom from Mexico, the war settled questions about Texas's boundaries.

der was the Nueces River, further north. When Texas joined the Union, the United States recognized the border as the Rio Grande.

After a short and unproductive attempt at *diplomacy*, troops under General Zachary Taylor crossed the Rio Grande and attacked Mexico. Congress declared war against Mexico on May 13, 1846. The war lasted two years and resulted in an overwhelming victory for America. The Mexicans were forced to give up California and New Mexico and recognize the Rio Grande as the border with Texas.

Texas was now the 28th state of the Union. In the years to come, its citizens recognized the contributions of the Alamo defenders to their independence and, later, their acceptance as citizens of the United States. For years, a company of Texas militiamen referred to themselves as the "Alamo Rifles."

Texas became known as the "Lone Star State." The state flag consists of two broad stripes: one red, the other white, as well as a field of blue containing a single star—a symbol of the willingness by Texans to stand alone for a just cause, just as the men of the Alamo stood alone in 1836. In fact, according to Davy Crockett's diary, a Lone Star flag flew at the Alamo.

On February 27, 1837, Colonel Juan Seguín, an officer in the Texas army, led a funeral procession to the Alamo. His men gathered the ashes of the Alamo defenders from the funeral *pyres* and had them buried. "They preferred a thousand deaths rather than surrender to serve the yoke of the tyrant," Seguín said. "What a brilliant example. Worthy indeed of being recorded in the pages of history. . . . I ask you to tell the world; Texas shall be free and independent or we shall perish with glory in battle."

> ## Make Connections
>
> Juan Seguín is known to have buried the ashes of the Alamo defenders, but the specific burial place on or near the grounds of the Alamo has never been found.

Text-Dependent Question
Why is Texas called the "Lone Star State?"

Research Project
San Antonio is one of the oldest European settlements in Texas. Do some research to find out more about the city's history before and after the Texas War for Independence.

Chronology

1723 Spaniards establish a mission near the town of San Antonio, Texas; later, the mission becomes known as the Alamo.

1821 Moses and Stephen F. Austin seek permission to establish an American colony in Texas; Mexico wins its independence from Spain.

1829 Mexico abolishes slavery to stem the flood of slave-owning Americans from entering Texas.

1830 Mexico enacts anti-American immigration laws, levies taxes on Texans and prohibits trade with the United States.

1831 Antonio López de Santa Anna takes office as president of Mexico; he later declares himself dictator.

1833 Stephen F. Austin is imprisoned in Mexico in January.

1835 Davy Crockett loses reelection to his seat in Congress and resolves to go to Texas; Stephen F. Austin is released from jail; Texans at Gonzales turn back an attack by Mexican troops on October 1, touching off the Texas War for Independence; Texans occupy the Alamo in December, and Jim Bowie and William Travis arrive to take command.

1836 Davy Crockett and a dozen frontiersmen from Tennessee arrive at the Alamo on February 8; Santa Anna's army of 5,500 men enter San Antonio on February 23 and the siege of the Alamo begins the next morning; the Alamo falls on March 6 after 183 defenders hold out for 11 days; Santa Anna is defeated April 21 at the battle of San Jacinto, and Texas wins its independence.

1845 Texas joins the Union as the 28th state on December 29.

1877 Part of the Alamo comes under private ownership when a merchant opens a general store in the Long Barracks.

1905 The Texas Legislature buys the Alamo and preserves it as a museum.

Series Glossary

capstone—a stone used at the top of a wall or other structure.

cornerstone—the first stone placed at a spot where two walls meet, usually considered the starting point of construction.

dome—an element of architecture that resembles the hollow upper half of a sphere.

edifice—a large building with an imposing appearance.

facade—the decorative front of a building.

foundation—the stone and mortar base built below ground that supports a building, bridge, monument, or other structure.

hallowed—holy, consecrated, sacred, or revered.

keystone—the architectural piece at the crown of a vault or arch which marks its apex, locking the other pieces into position.

memorial—something designed to help people remember a person or event in history.

obelisk—a shaft of stone that tapers at the peak.

pantheon—a public building containing monuments to a nation's heroes.

pedestal—the base or support on which a statue, obelisk, or column is mounted.

portico—a roof supported by columns, usually extending out from a building.

rotunda—a large and high circular hall or room in a building, usually surmounted by a dome.

standard—a flag or banner that is adopted as an emblem or symbol by a nation.

symbol—an item that represents or stands for something else.

Further Reading

Belviso, Meg, and Pam Pollack. *What Was the Alamo?* Illus. by David Groff. New York: Grosset and Dunlap, 2013.

Donovan, James. *The Blood of Heroes: The 13-Day Struggle for the Alamo—and the Sacrifice That Forged a Nation.* New York: Little, Brown and Co., 2012.

Roberts, Randy, and James C. Olson. *A Line in the Sand: The Alamo in Blood and Memory.* New York: Free Press, 2001.

Sorrels, Roy. *The Legend of the Alamo.* Berkeley Heights, N.J.: Enslow Publishers, 2013.

Wallis, Michael. *David Crockett: The Lion of the West.* New York: W.W. Norton, 2011.

Internet Resources

www.thealamo.org/main/index.php

The official website of the Alamo provides news and information about the landmark site, links to resources for students and teachers, and other information.

www.tshaonline.org/handbook/online/articles/qea02

The Texas State Historical Association provides information about the battle of the Alamo, with links to information about relevant people and events from Texas history.

www.tsl.state.tx.us/treasures/republic/alamo-01.html

The Texas State Library and Archives has posted information, documents, and images related to the war for Texas independence at this site.

Index

Index

Picture Credits

Contributors

BARRY MORENO has been librarian and historian at the Ellis Island Immigration Museum and the Statue of Liberty National Monument since 1988. *The Statue of Liberty Encyclopedia* (2000), *The Encyclopedia of Ellis Island* (2004), *Ellis Island's Famous Immigrants* (2008), and *The Ellis Island Quiz Book* (2011). He also co-edited a scholarly study on world migration called *Leaving Home: Migration Yesterday and Today* (2011). His biography has been included in *Who's Who Among Hispanic Americans*, *The Directory of National Park Service Historians*, *Who's Who in America*, and *The Directory of American Scholars*. Mr. Moreno lives in New York City.

HAL MARCOVITZ has written more than 100 books for young readers. He lives in Chalfont, Pennsylvania, with his wife, Gail. They have two grown daughters, Ashley and Michelle.